MAR 2019

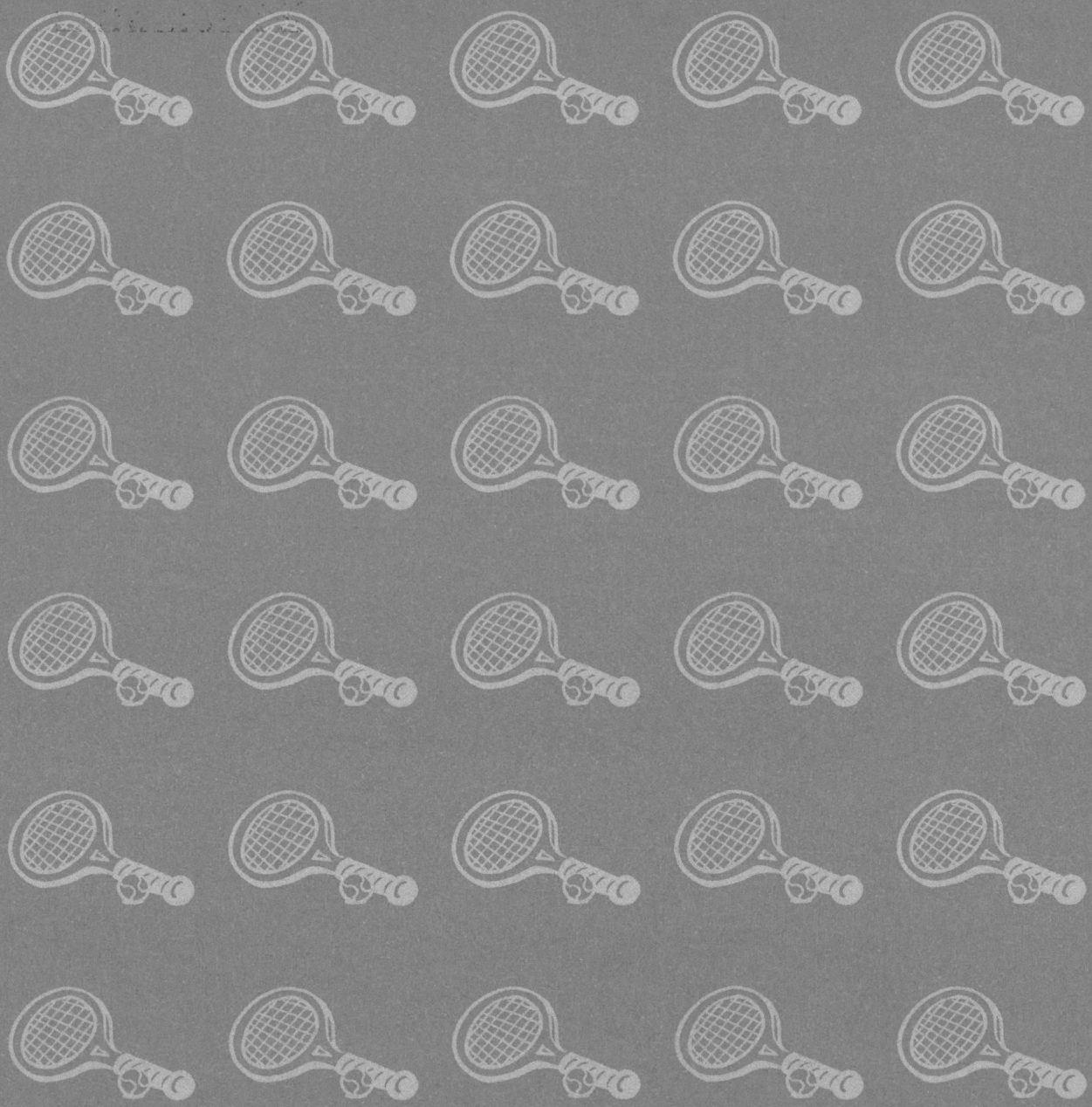

CHARLESTON COUNTY LIBRARY
WITHDRAWN

ORDINARY PEOPLE CHANGE the WORLD

I am Billie Jean King

BRAD MELTZER
illustrated by Christopher Eliopoulos

DIAL BOOKS FOR YOUNG READERS

I am Billie Jean King.

Fair play.

It's such a simple idea.

In sports and in life, it means you respect the rules and treat everyone equally.

But sometimes people don't want to play fair.

And other times, they don't even want to let you play.

But that never stopped me.

When I was little, people called me a tomboy, which is a word I still don't like.

Girls can enjoy sports just as much as boys.

Today, many dads encourage their daughters to play sports.
But back when I was growing up, my dad was one of the first.
Most important, he played equally with both me and my brother.
Equal time.
Equal respect.

I was so good at baseball, my dream was to be a professional player.
But when I went to my first real baseball game, I noticed something.

It didn't seem fair.
I'd have to find another sport.

Fortunately, in fifth grade a friend asked me a question that changed my life.

My first time on the court, I had no idea what I was doing.

Back then, tennis was a game played mostly by wealthy people at fancy country clubs.

That wasn't my family. My mother sewed my white shorts; my racquet was borrowed.

DID I MISS A FEW SHOTS?

SURE. NO ONE IS INSTANTLY AN EXPERT.

BEING A GREAT PLAYER TAKES HARD WORK.

A few weeks later, I heard about a coach named Clyde Walker, who gave free coaching on the public courts.

Often, the right teacher can change your life.

Coach Clyde taught me how to hold the racquet. And he made tennis *fun*.

That first afternoon, I was hooked.

I had found the sport I loved.

When my mom came to pick me up, I told her...

Now I just needed the right equipment.

To save money for a tennis racquet, I did odd jobs around the neighborhood, like taking out people's trash and weeding their gardens.

As a city employee, Coach Clyde traveled to a different park every day.

My mom drove me for hours to get his free coaching, all across Long Beach, California.

Mom didn't drive me because she thought I'd be rich.

Back then, playing tennis didn't pay much money, especially if you were a woman.

She drove me so I could do what I loved.

Not everyone cheered me on.

At one tournament, they wouldn't let me be in the group photo.

By the time I was twelve years old, at the fancy L.A. Tennis Club, I noticed something else: Everyone wore white . . . and everyone *was* white.

I wanted things to change.

Tennis shouldn't be a sport only for rich white people.

It should be a sport everyone can enjoy.

Every day, I worked with Coach Clyde.

I also worked at home.

My brother would practice pitching baseballs, and I'd make sure my tennis serves didn't knock over any lamps.

At fifteen, I had to write an essay about my future.

At sixteen, I started being coached by Alice Marble, a former number one tennis player who won eighteen Grand Slam championships, which are the biggest events of all.

She convinced me I could win—and made me realize how many strong women in sports had come before me.

I was part of something bigger than just myself.

Soon, a new thing also started happening.

With Coach Alice, I went from number nineteen in the country to number four.

By age seventeen, I made it all the way to Wimbledon.

We won the women's doubles title, which is when you play tennis with a partner.

We were the youngest team to ever do it.

We couldn't afford to go to the big Wimbledon celebration ball.

But we enjoyed the victory.

As I started college, I was ranked number three in the country, but my school still didn't give me a scholarship.

Over the years, even as my career moved forward, people still didn't treat women equally.

When a man won a tournament, he'd get a big check.

When a woman won the same tournament, she was paid much less.

When a man won, the reporters would ask him questions about the match.

When a woman won, they'd ask...

People would tell me that's just how the world worked.

Women were paid less than men.

They were treated worse than men.

I knew I had to change it.

Soon, I achieved one of the greatest victories of my career.

After winning Wimbledon a second time—in singles, doubles, and mixed doubles (which is when men and women play together)—I thought things would get better for women.

They didn't.

There were so many tennis greats who came before me—

Each of them taught me something. It's like they were there with me, on one team.

I was the number one player in the world, but I was being paid so little, I couldn't even get a credit card.

It was time to take action.

When tournaments didn't offer equal pay, we started protesting.

They called us The Original Nine.

Thanks to our women's tour, tournament organizers quickly realized fans would pay just as much to see us play.

Soon after, I was the first woman ever named *Sports Illustrated*'s Sportsperson of the Year.

But with every step forward, there was always someone who wanted to move things back.

His name was Bobby Riggs.

At one point in time, he was the number one tennis player in the world.

Now he was fifty-five years old and a loudmouthed bully.

Bobby Riggs insisted women weren't as strong as men.
To prove it, he challenged me to a match.
When I refused, he challenged Margaret Court, who had recently become the number one female player in the world.
I'M GOING TO PLAY HIM, BILLIE JEAN.
WHAT?
THEY'RE PAYING ME $10,000.
FIRST, THAT'S NOT ENOUGH.
SECOND, YOU NEED TO WIN THIS MATCH, MARGARET!
EVERYONE WILL BE WATCHING.
THEY'LL WANT TO SEE IF WE'RE AS STRONG AS MEN.
IT'S THE MATCH OF THE CENTURY!
MAN VERSUS WOMAN!
GET READY TO SEE WOMEN LOSE!

They played on Mother's Day.
You had to win two out of three sets.
Bobby beat Margaret.
Easily.

I heard the score in an airport.

My reaction was instantaneous.

It was called the Battle of the Sexes, the biggest tennis match the world had ever seen.

I knew what was at stake.

Bobby treated it like it'd be easy.

The match was set at the Astrodome, a massive stadium in Texas.

Since it had a white roof, I knew it would be hard to see the tennis ball when it was up high in the lights.

I also knew Bobby liked to hit them high, so for weeks, I practiced hitting 150 overhead shots *every single day.*

Instead of playing best of three, which was what women usually played, we decided to play best of five.

The prize money was a record-setting $100,000, winner take all.

Around this time, I also realized I was gay.

Being gay means that if you're a girl, you love and have romantic feelings for other girls—and if you're a boy, you love and have romantic feelings for other boys.

If I lost the match, I knew it would erase everything I'd achieved in tennis.

But I was ready to win.

In fact, the night before, I called my brother and told him to place a bet.

On the big day, I went over my game plan and did the most important thing of all:

I read through the hundreds of letters that had come that week from fans.

This wasn't just a tennis match.

It was a fight to prove how strong women were.

Little girls around the country were counting on me.

On September 20, 1973, 30,000 fans packed the Astrodome.

Ninety million more were watching on TV, which is more than some Super Bowls.

To this day, it is the most watched tennis match *ever*.

This was the big time.
The world was watching.
Now I just had to deliver the right statement.

At the beginning of the match, Bobby was wearing a jacket.

He was slower than I thought he'd be.

Bobby wasn't talking or bragging anymore. He was scared, breathing heavily.

He was just another bully. And every bully can be defeated.

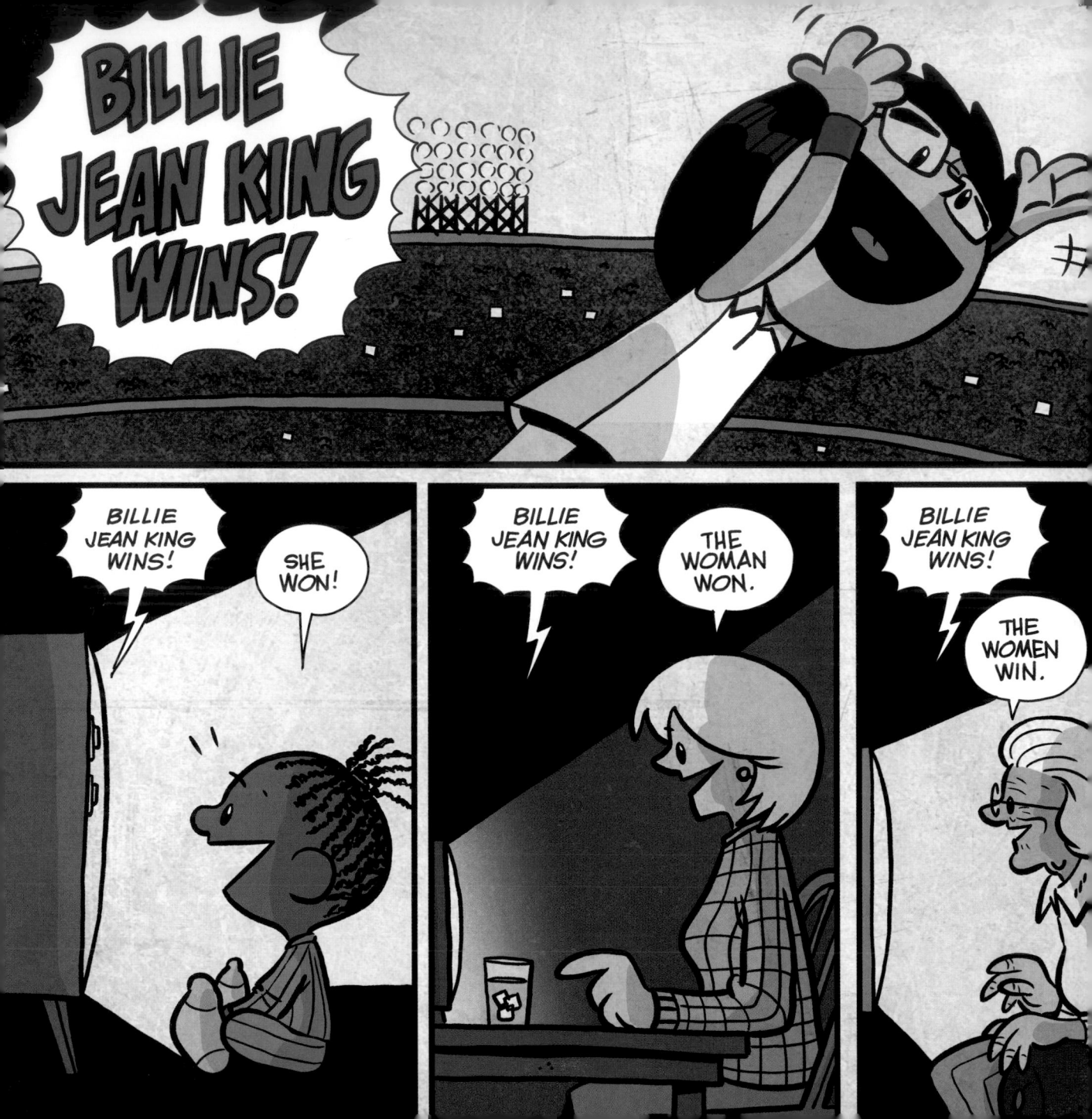
BILLIE JEAN KING WINS!
BILLIE JEAN KING WINS!
SHE WON!
BILLIE JEAN KING WINS!
THE WOMAN WON.
BILLIE JEAN KING WINS!
THE WOMEN WIN.

I crushed him in three straight sets: 6–4, 6–3, 6–3.
He didn't win a single one.
BILLIE JEAN KING WINS!
WE WON!
For millions, it was the very first time they'd seen a woman beat a man at anything.
Riggs jumped over the net to congratulate me.
The first words he said were . . .
I UNDERESTIMATED YOU.
He did.

After my victory, I testified before Congress on the Education Equality Act, which would fund the goals of Title IX and make sure that girls' sports got the same amount of money as boys' sports.

Even after Larry and I stopped being married, we still stayed close. The two of us established World Team Tennis, where men and women would play on the same team.
Together.
As equals.
ONE OF THE BEST PARTS OF WORLD TEAM TENNIS WERE THESE CLINICS,
WHICH WE OFFERED TO KIDS, INCLUDING THIS EIGHT-YEAR-OLD GIRL AND HER LITTLE SISTER.
I'M VENUS WILLIAMS.
I'M SERENA.
OUR DAD SAW YOU PLAY ON TV AND DECIDED HIS DAUGHTERS SHOULD PLAY TENNIS TOO.
NICE TO MEET YOU, VENUS AND SERENA.

In my life, people expected me to dress like a girl.
Act like a girl.
And hit like one.
I did.
I *always* hit the ball like a girl, which means harder and more powerfully than anyone.

All of us are powerful in our own ways.
So how do you get to be your best self?
By practicing, sweating, and giving everything you've got.
And when you have nothing left, give more.

BEFORE THE BATTLE OF THE SEXES, ONLY ONE IN TWENTY-SEVEN GIRLS PLAYED A HIGH SCHOOL SPORT. BY THE END OF THE DECADE, ONE IN THREE DID.
TODAY, THE U.S. TENNIS ASSOCIATION FACILITY IN NEW YORK IS CALLED THE BILLIE JEAN KING NATIONAL TENNIS CENTER.
THE COURTS ARE OPEN TO THE PUBLIC—JUST LIKE THE ONES SHE LEARNED ON.
42

IN 2009, PRESIDENT OBAMA MADE HER THE FIRST FEMALE ATHLETE TO WIN THE PRESIDENTIAL MEDAL OF FREEDOM,
FOR BEING ONE OF THE FIRST OPENLY LESBIAN SPORTS FIGURES, AND FOR USING SPORTS TO CREATE SOCIAL CHANGE.
THE BEST IS STILL TO COME.
I LOOK FORWARD TO SEEING A WOMAN PLAY BASEBALL IN THE WORLD SERIES AT SOME POINT IN MY LIFETIME.

Playing fair is the same in both sports and life.

If everyone doesn't get the same chance, you'll never find out who's truly the best.

Real victory doesn't come from points scored.

It comes from how you treat others in the game.

No one really wins until everyone gets to play.

BJK
BJK
BJK
allan

"Be bold. If you're going to make an error, make a doozy, and don't be afraid to hit the ball."
—Billie Jean King

Timeline

NOVEMBER 22, 1943	1961–1964	1961	SEPTEMBER 17, 1965	1966	1966, 1967, 1968, 1971, 1972, 1974
Born in Long Beach, California	Attends California State University	Wins first doubles title at Wimbledon	Marries Larry King	Wins first singles title at Wimbledon	Is ranked number one in women's tennis

Billie Jean with her father

Billie Jean as Grand Marshall of the NYC Pride Parade, 2018

Billie Jean and Bobby Riggs before the Battle of the Sexes

Winning Wimbledon in 1972

Billie Jean and her partner, Ilana Kloss

1970
The Original Nine and the birth of women's pro tennis

1972
Wins three Grand Slams (French Open, U.S. Open, and Wimbledon) in same year

SEPTEMBER 20, 1973
Wins Battle of the Sexes tennis match

1973
Forms the Women's Tennis Association

1979
Starts dating life partner Ilana Kloss

2009
Receives the Presidential Medal of Freedom

For my Aunt Debbie,
one of my favorite sports fans,
as well as our other LGBTQ friends and family,
whom we love and support
for being exactly who they are
—B.M.

For Elizabeth, Alexa, Megan, Christopher, and Jennifer Rand.
They make my life more fun!
—C.E.

For historical accuracy, we used Billie Jean King's actual dialogue whenever possible. For more of Ms. King's true voice, we recommend and acknowledge the below titles. Special thanks to the inspiring and amazing Billie Jean King—as well as the generous Tip Nunn—for their input on early drafts (and for all the photo references too).

SOURCES

Autobiography of Billie Jean King by Billie Jean King (HarperCollins, 1982)

Billie Jean by Billie Jean King with Frank Deford (Viking, 1982)

Pressure Is a Privilege by Billie Jean King with Christine Brennan (LifeTime Media, Inc., 2008)

Game, Set, Match: Billie Jean King and the Revolution in Women's Sports by Susan Ware (UNC Press, 2011)

PBS American Masters documentary, 2013: http://www.pbs.org/wnet/americanmasters/billie-jean-king-film-billie-jean-king/2637/

Publisher's Letter by Billie Jean King, *womenSports* magazine, August 1977

FURTHER READING FOR KIDS

Good Night Stories for Rebel Girls 2 by Elena Favilli and Francesca Cavallo (Timbuktu Labs, 2018)

Women in Sports: 50 Fearless Athletes Who Played to Win by Rachel Ignotofsky (Ten Speed Press, 2017)

DIAL BOOKS FOR YOUNG READERS
Penguin Young Readers Group • An imprint of Penguin Random House LLC • 375 Hudson Street, New York, NY 10014

Text copyright © 2019 by Forty-four Steps, Inc. • Illustrations copyright © 2019 by Christopher Eliopoulos

Penguin supports copyright. Copyright fuels creativity, encourages diverse voices, promotes free speech, and creates a vibrant culture. Thank you for buying an authorized edition of this book and for complying with copyright laws by not reproducing, scanning, or distributing any part of it in any form without permission. You are supporting writers and allowing Penguin to continue to publish books for every reader.

Library of Congress Cataloging-in-Publication Data
Names: Meltzer, Brad, author. | Eliopoulos, Chris, illustrator. • Title: I am Billie Jean King / by Brad Meltzer ; illustrated by Christopher Eliopoulos.
Description: New York : Dial Books for Young Readers, an imprint of Penguin Random House, LLC [2019] | Series: Ordinary People Change the World |
Audience: Ages: 5–8. | Audience: Grades: K to Grade 3. • Identifiers: LCCN 2018031285 | ISBN 9780735228740 (hardcover)
Subjects: LCSH: King, Billie Jean—Juvenile literature. | Women tennis players—United States—Biography—Juvenile literature. | Tennis players—United States—Biography—Juvenile literature. • Classification: LCC GV994.K56 M45 2019 | DDC 796.342092 [B]—dc23 LC record available at https://lccn.loc.gov/2018031285

Portrait of Billie Jean King (page 38) and photo of Billie Jean with Bobby Riggs (page 39) courtesy of Bettman/Getty Images. Photo of Billie Jean with her father (page 39) courtesy of Billie Jean King. Photo of the NYC Pride Parade (page 39) courtesy of Steven Ferdman/Stringer/Getty Images. Photo at Wimbledon (page 39) courtesy of Evening Standard/Stringer/Getty Images. Photo of Billie Jean with Ilana Kloss (page 39) courtesy of Michael Tran/Getty Images.

Printed in China • 10 9 8 7 6 5 4 3 2 1
Designed by Jason Henry • Text set in Triplex • The artwork for this book was created digitally.